BODIES OF WATER
LAKES

A Crabtree Roots Book

DOUGLAS BENDER

CRABTREE
Publishing Company
www.crabtreebooks.com

School-to-Home Support for Caregivers and Teachers

This book helps children grow by letting them practice reading. Here are a few guiding questions to help the reader with building his or her comprehension skills. Possible answers appear here in red.

Before Reading:
- What do I think this book is about?
  - *I think this book is about how lakes are made.*
  - *I think this book is about lakes and what they look like.*
- What do I want to learn about this topic?
  - *I want to learn what animals live in lakes.*
  - *I want to learn how lakes are made.*

During Reading:
- I wonder why...
  - *I wonder why fish live in lakes.*
  - *I wonder why holes are made in the ground.*
- What have I learned so far?
  - *I have learned that people can swim in lakes.*
  - *I have learned that plants and animals can live in and around lakes.*

After Reading:
- What details did I learn about this topic?
  - *I have learned that lakes can be big or small in size.*
  - *I have learned that lakes are surrounded by land.*
- Read the book again and look for the vocabulary words.
  - *I see the word **holes** on page 4 and the word **shores** on page 12. The other vocabulary words are found on page 14.*

This is a **lake**.

Lakes are made from big **holes**.

You can find fish
in lakes.

You can find **plants** in lakes.

People can **swim** in lakes.

All lakes have **shores**.

Word List
Sight Words

a	find	is
all	fish	made
are	from	this
big	have	you
can	in	

Words to Know

holes

lake

plants

shores

swim

31 Words

This is a **lake**.

Lakes are made from big **holes**.

You can find fish in lakes.

You can find **plants** in lakes.

People can **swim** in lakes.

All lakes have **shores**.

CRABTREE
Publishing Company

Written by: Douglas Bender
Designed by: Rhea Wallace
Series Development: James Earley
Proofreader: Janine Deschenes
Educational Consultant: Marie Lemke M.Ed.

Photographs:
Shutterstock: digidreamgrafix: cover; Songquan Deng: p. 1; Elena Elisseeva: p. 3, 14; a4ndreas: p. 4-5; evronphoto: p. 6; LianeM: p. 9, 14; ZsoltBiczo: p. 11, 14; Alex Stemmer: p. 13, 14

Library and Archives
Canada Cataloguing in Publication

Title: Lakes / Douglas Bender.
Names: Bender, Douglas, 1992- author.
Description: Series statement: Bodies of water | "A Crabtree roots book".
Identifiers: Canadiana (print) 20210190248 |
    Canadiana (ebook) 20210190361 |
    ISBN 9781427155917 (hardcover) |
    ISBN 9781427155979 (softcover) |
    ISBN 9781427133830 (HTML) |
    ISBN 9781427134431 (EPUB) |
    ISBN 9781427156150 (read-along ebook)
Subjects: LCSH: Lakes—Juvenile literature.
Classification: LCC GB1603.8 .B46 2022 | DDC j551.48/2—dc23

Library of Congress
Cataloging-in-Publication Data

Names: Bender, Douglas, 1992- author.
Title: Lakes / Douglas Bender.
Description: New York, NY : Crabtree Publishing, [2022] |
    Series: Bodies of water - a Crabtree roots book |
    Includes index.
Identifiers: LCCN 2021017104 (print) | LCCN 2021017105 (ebook) |
    ISBN 9781427155917 (hardcover) |
    ISBN 9781427155979 (paperback) |
    ISBN 9781427133830 (ebook) |
    ISBN 9781427134431 (epub) | ISBN 9781427156150
Subjects: LCSH: Lakes--Juvenile literature.
Classification: LCC GB1603.8 .B45 2022 (print) | LCC GB1603.8 (ebook) | DDC 551.48/2--dc23
LC record available at https://lccn.loc.gov/2021017104
LC ebook record available at https://lccn.loc.gov/2021017105

Crabtree Publishing Company

www.crabtreebooks.com   1-800-387-7650   Printed in the U.S.A./062021/CG20210401

Published in the United States
Crabtree Publishing
347 Fifth Avenue, Suite 1402-145
New York, NY, 10016

Published in Canada
Crabtree Publishing
616 Welland Ave.
St. Catharines, Ontario L2M 5V6